Prague Self-Guided Walks: Prague Castle

KRYSTI BRICE

DEDICATION

This series of Prague Self-Guided Walks is dedicated to my mother, who helped me immensely in creating them.

CONTENTS

ACKNOWLEDGMENTS

Heartfelt thanks go out to my teachers of art history,
Theopisti and Hana; to Iva for her tireless support of all of
my projects; and to Sarah for her interest in my books
about Prague.

1 INTRODUCTION

Prague, the city of a thousand spires and more than a thousand years of history, the city of alchemists and Kafka, the city that Mozart loved, is one of the most beautiful and mysterious in the world. Having escaped with very little damage in World War II, it has one of the few almost fully-intact historical city centers in Europe.

The old center of Prague is quite expansive, having grown more or less organically from its medieval origins like the layers of an onion. Wandering through its streets, you will get the sense that the beauty and the history never end. Except for the crowds of tourists, the ubiquity of souvenir shops and the newness of the buildings' refurbished facades, Prague looks much as it did several centuries ago. Here it is possible to get lost in time, especially if you get off the main drags and onto some of the city's winding side streets.

If you like to venture into a new city on your own, this walking guide will help you do just that, showing you the way through one of the oldest areas of Prague: Prague Castle (Pražský Hrad or Hradčany).

Prague Castle ("the Castle"), sitting as it does atop a bluff overlooking the Vltava (Moldau) River, dominates the skyline of the city. Prague "Castle" is really somewhat of a misnomer, as it is not really one "castle" or structure, but rather a collection of buildings that began as a fortress and grew into a community that eventually became one of Prague's five original "towns." (The others are: Old Town, New Town, the Lesser Quarter or Malá Strana, and the Jewish Quarter.) This somewhat misleading name, combined with the uniform appearance of the Castle's 18th-century edifice (when viewed from the river below), gives the impression that Prague Castle is a single building to be visited like a museum or palace. But that would be to miss the rich history contained within the complex that is hidden by that lovely yet uniform edifice which Queen Maria Theresa commissioned when she ruled Austro-Hungary.

Prague Castle comprises buildings dating back to the 9th century. In fact, it is the part of Prague that contains the city's oldest structures and remnants. The Czech founding Přemyslid dynasty chose this strategic location above the river for their kingdom's original fortress, and since the 11th century, Prague Castle has been the official seat of Bohemian kings and princes, then of Czechoslovak presidents, and then of Czech presidents until today (and the seat of a few Holy Roman Emperors, too).

2 SOME PRAGUE HISTORY

Czech history is extremely complex, as is Prague's. So for the purposes of this walk, I'll try to keep it brief and relatively simple.

Prague, the capital of the Czech Republic and of the lands historically known as Bohemia (or the Czech lands), was founded when the Czech Slavic tribes were unified under the Přemyslid dynasty during the Romanesque period. The other regions that make up the Czech Republic are Moravia and Silesia.

Over the centuries following its founding, Prague has had mixed fortunes, at times being independent but most often being under the yoke of other lands. Although it has long been an important center in the heart of Europe, two periods in particular stand out as times during which Prague flourished and experienced great prosperity and importance. These were the 14th and the 16th centuries, under the reigns of Charles IV and Rudolf II, respectively, when Prague was not only the capital of Bohemia but was also the seat of the Holy Roman Empire.

Jan Hus was a Czech protestant reformer who predated Martin Luther by a century (in fact, Luther was inspired by Hus). His reform movement sparked the Hussite Wars which erupted a decade or so after Hus was burned at the stake for heresy in 1415. Knowing he would otherwise burn, Hus was given a chance to recant all he had said about the excesses of the Catholic Church, yet he chose to stand for his beliefs and face the fire. For this reason, I believe that we all owe a debt to Jan Hus.

From Hus's death until 1620, Bohemia was the site of many protestant uprisings. The so-called Second Defenestration of Prague in 1618, when two Catholic officials and their secretary were thrown out of a window at Prague Castle by Protestant rebels, is credited with starting the Thirty Years' War.

Early in that war, the Czech Protestant armies were soundly defeated by the Hapsburg Catholics at the Battle of White Mountain. Subsequently, Prague and the Czech lands fell under the firm grip of the Hapsburgs (until World War I), and the Counterreformation ensued. In Prague and the Czech lands, this meant (among other things) inundating the territory and the capital with Baroque architecture in an effort to re-Catholicize the population.

Resistant to religion in general and to Catholicism in particular after so many centuries of religious strife and foreign (i.e., Catholic in Czech minds) occupation, the Czechs were a hard sell when it came to all religion but especially when it came to Catholicism. So the Baroque style, with its beauty and drama, was seen as a perfect propaganda tool in the Hapsburgs' attempt to bring the population back into the Catholic fold. The Baroque was meant to impress, overwhelm and brag – and it does. Especially in the Czech lands, where the population was

90% protestant by the time the Thirty Years' War broke out, extra persuasion was needed. For that reason, Baroque architecture dominates Prague and the entire Czech Republic (with rare exception, every Czech town and village has at least one richly decorated Baroque church in its center), and the Baroque of Bohemia is particularly intense.

And if Czechs were going to be "persuaded" to be Catholic, they were going to need to be able to understand "Catholic" music (Baroque music at the time), reasoned the powers that were. So the Hapsburgs instituted a program of music instruction for all Czech schoolchildren. This had the effect of creating a land of very musically-literate and -talented people, and this is one reason you will notice that classical music concerts, most of quite high quality, are ubiquitous in Prague.

During the Counterreformation, much of Prague's Old Town was remodeled in the Baroque style. But while Old Town got a mere facelift, the Lesser Quarter (Malá Strana) was nearly completely rebuilt in a Baroque building boom. Due to its proximity to Prague Castle, the Malá Strana was the neighborhood of choice for the noble families of the Czech and other Hapsburg lands who wished to reside close to the Castle and to the seat of power. So after the Catholic armies' victories in the Thirty Years' War, land in the Malá Strana was given to noble families, victorious generals and various orders of the Catholic Church who proceeded to build grand palaces, gardens, churches and monasteries on it.

From the 16th to the 20th centuries, Prague and the Czech lands were part of the Austro-Hungarian Empire. When that empire dissolved after World War I, the country of Czechoslovakia was founded, with Prague as its capital. World War II brought Nazi occupation and the decimation of the country's Jewish population, followed by forty years of Communist rule that eventually included occupation by Soviet troops beginning in 1968. In 1989, the fall of the Berlin Wall brought freedom, followed shortly thereafter by the breakup of Czechoslovakia and the formation of the Czech Republic in 1993. (The Soviet troops took their time leaving – the last of the soldiers departed in 1991, some 23 years after they rolled onto Wenceslas Square, and two years after the fall of the Communist regime.)

Historically, Prague was made up of five smaller, formerly independent (not totally independent, but rather like the boroughs of New York City) towns that are now unified: Prague Castle (Hradčany), Old Town (Staré Město), the Jewish Quarter (Josefov), the Lesser Quarter or Little Town (Malá Strana) and New Town (Nové Město).

Because each of these towns had its own city administration, mayor, town hall, guilds and purpose, each of them developed separately and therefore differently from the others, which is evident even today in each area's architecture and atmosphere. And as I mentioned in the Introduction, Prague never suffered significant damage in any war, which means it escaped the especially destructive capability of the weaponry available in World War II. Combined, all of these factors meant that an opportunity to impose a "unified vision" of a grand, "modern" city onto Prague never really presented itself. Even the layout of the streets in the historic center is the result of medieval town planning, which you'll sense as you walk around the unique city that exists today.

3 MAPS

I've provided several maps, including a general overview of the layout of Prague and detailed maps of various areas of Prague Castle and some of its structures. I have done my best to make them as self-explanatory as possible. However, as you can appreciate, it is difficult to get the right level of detail to appear in the space of one page of a small book. So you might also ask for a map at your hotel or pension, which normally provide them for free. And, of course, you can use your smartphone!

Map 1: General Overview of Prague

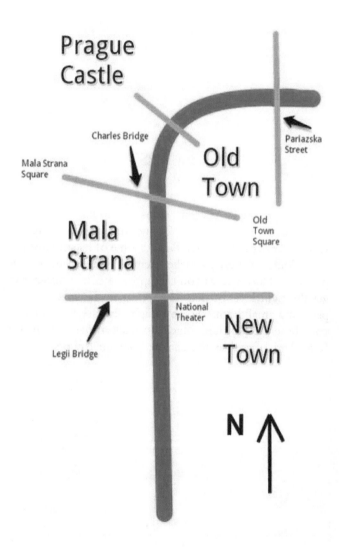

Map 2: Overview of Prague Castle and Starting Points

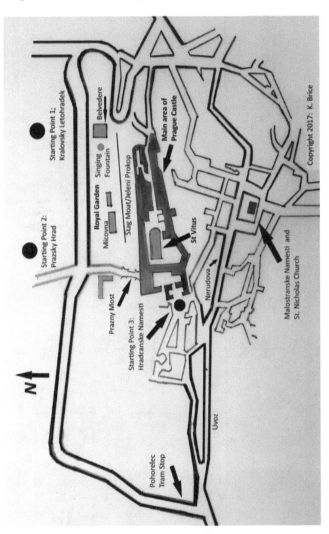

Map 3: Starting Points 1 and 2 – the Royal Garden and Powder Bridge

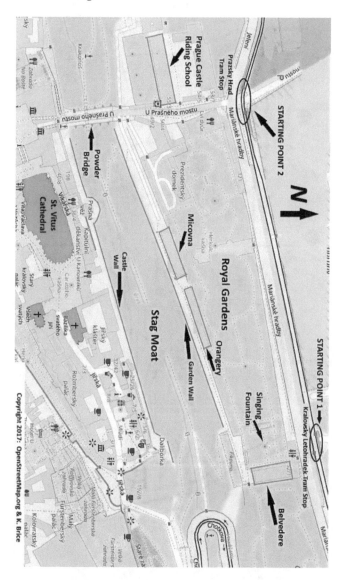

Map 4: Starting Point 3 – Hradčanské Náměstí

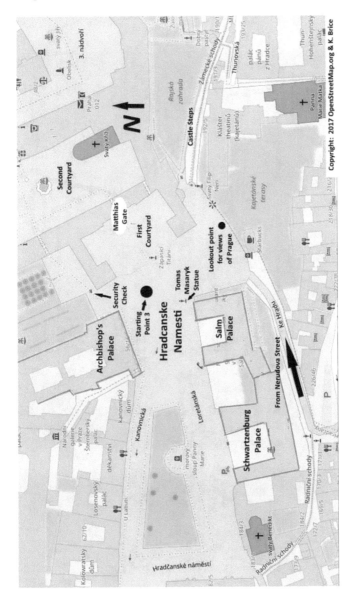

Map 5: Starting Point 3 – The Second Courtyard

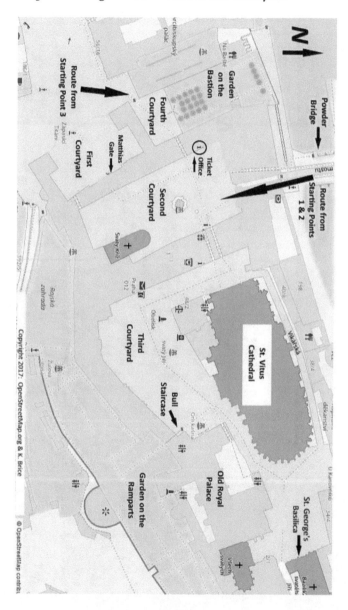

Map 6: St. Vitus Cathedral

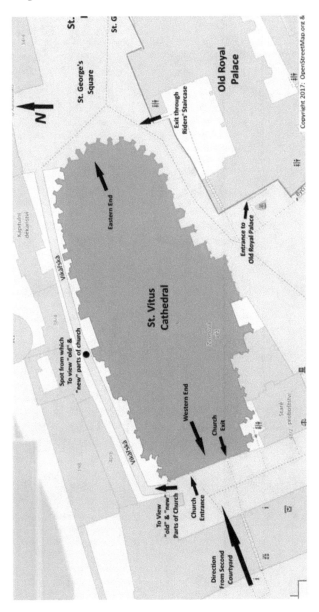

Map 7: St. George's Basilica and Golden Lane

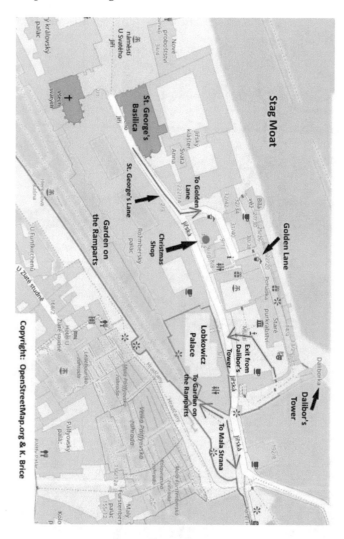

Map 8: Detail of St. Vitus Cathedral

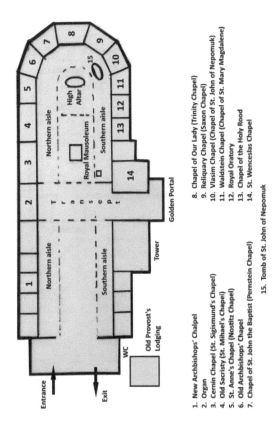

1. New Archbishops' Chalpel
2. Organ
3. Cernin Chapel (St. Sigismund's Chapel)
4. Old Sacristy (St. Mihael's Chapel)
5. St. Anne's Chapel (Nostitz Chapel)
6. Old Archbishops' Chapel
7. Chapel of St. John the Baptist (Pernstein Chapel)

8. Chapel of Our Lady (Trinity Chapel)
9. Reliquary Chapel (Saxon Chapel)
10. Vlasim Chapel (Chapel of St. John of Nepomuk)
11. Waldstein Chapel (Chapel of St. Mary Magdalene)
12. Royal Oratory
13. Chapel of the Holy Rood
14. St. Wenceslas Chapel

15. Tomb of St. John of Nepomuk

Copyright 2017: K. Brice

Map 9: Detail of the Old Royal Palace

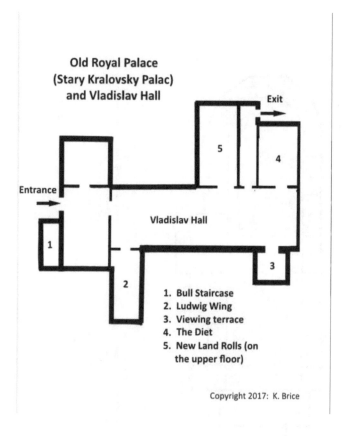

Old Royal Palace
(Stary Kralovsky Palac)
and Vladislav Hall

Exit

Entrance

5

4

Vladislav Hall

1

3

2

1. Bull Staircase
2. Ludwig Wing
3. Viewing terrace
4. The Diet
5. New Land Rolls (on
   the upper floor)

Copyright 2017: K. Brice

Map 10: Detail of St. George's Basilica

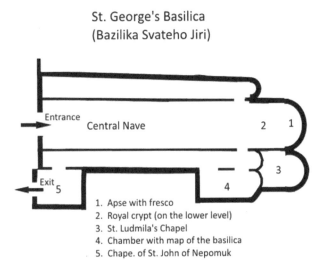

St. George's Basilica
(Bazilika Svateho Jiri)

1. Apse with fresco
2. Royal crypt (on the lower level)
3. St. Ludmila's Chapel
4. Chamber with map of the basilica
5. Chape. of St. John of Nepomuk

Copyright 2017: K. Brice

4 OVERVIEW OF THE PRAGUE CASTLE WALK

There are many ways to get to Prague Castle and thus many starting points for this self-guided walk. I'll describe three of them, and then you can decide which one suits your plans (and your stamina) best.

Note: For all of the routes below, take extra care when crossing the tram tracks – the trams have right of way, and anyway, they weigh 20 tons, so you don't want to challenge them. Cars are supposed to stop at zebra crossings, but be sure the driver has noticed you and is slowing down before you step out into one.

Starting Point 1: The Royal Garden and the Royal Summer Palace (Belvedere)
To get here: Take tram number 22 to the stop "Kralovský Letohradek"

If you are in Prague between April 1 and October 31 and you like gardens, you might want to start this walk at the Royal Garden (note that from November 1 to March 31 each year, the gardens are closed; also, this garden is occasionally used for various local festivals which require an entry fee). When you exit the tram at Pražský Letohradek, look for the gates across the street from the tram stop. Just beyond them you'll see the green, swooping roof of a gorgeous Renaissance building. Enter through the gates and begin the walk as laid out at the beginning of Chapter 5 – Starting Point 1.

Tip: Take advantage of the restrooms on the right just after you enter the gate if you are in need. Another opportunity will not present itself for a while. You'll need CZK 10.

Starting Point 2: Powder Bridge (Prašný Most)
To get here: Take tram number 22 to the stop "Pražský Hrad"

If you don't fancy gardens, or if you are short of time or are in Prague between November 1 and March 31 when all gardens in Prague are closed, continue one more stop past Pražský Letohradek (if you're coming up from town) on tram 22 to the stop "Pražský Hrad." When you exit the tram, cross the tram tracks and the street running parallel to them (you'll be walking south as you cross) and enter the Castle grounds on the street U Prašného Mostu. Proceed to Prašný Most (the Powder Bridge) and pick up the tour at the Prague Castle Riding School.

Tip: The ride up to the Castle on tram 22 will present you with beautiful views of the old historical center of the city out of the right-hand side of the tram on your way up, and out the left-hand side if you choose to ride back down when you finish this walk.

Starting Point 3: Prague Castle Gates on Hradčanské Náměstí

To get here: Walk up Nerudova Street from Malostranské Náměstí. Take tram 12, 15, 20 or 22 to the stop Malostranské Náměstí.

If you have a lot of stamina, or if you just want some good exercise to work off all the beer and dumplings you've had since arriving in Prague, you can walk up Nerudova Street from Malostranské Náměstí, turning sharply on the hairpin turn to the right onto Ke Hradu, and on up to the gates of Prague Castle. If you take this route, begin the tour at Hradčanské Náměstí.

Another way to reach this spot is to take the 22 tram to the stop Pohořelec and walk downhill on Loretánská Street to Hradčanské Náměstí where you will see the gates of Prague Castle.

Tickets

It is possible to visit the grounds of Prague Castle without buying any ticket at all. You can enter the grounds and stroll through them anytime from 6:00 a.m. until 10:00 p.m.

However, in order to visit the **interiors** of the sites of Prague Castle, including the ones covered in this walk, you will have to buy one of two tickets: a "long visit" or a "short visit." **This book covers the four sites included in the "short visit" ticket, or "Circuit B" at the ticket office:**

1. St. Vitus Cathedral,
2. The Old Royal Palace,
3. St. George's Basilica, and
4. Golden Lane with Dalibor's Tower.

You will be directed to the ticket office in the text that follows for the routes from each starting point.

The interiors of the historical buildings are open as follows:

- April 1 till October 31 – 9:00 a.m. to 5:00 p.m.
- November 1 till March 31 – 9:00 a.m. to 4:00 p.m.

Note that St. Vitus Cathedral's opening hours vary slightly from the above at certain times. It is a functioning church and has weekly services, so on Sundays it opens at 12:00 p.m. **In addition, the last entry is always 20 minutes before the official closing time year-round.**

At other times special services or a wedding or funeral for VIPs are held in St. Vitus, but they are unpredictable (though fortunately rare). So, if you have the misfortune of finding the church closed when you arrive, hopefully it will not be closed for the entire day, and you will get a chance to tour it on your visit.

Another exception is the Prague Castle Gardens, which do not open until 10:00 a.m. And, again, remember that all gardens at the Castle and elsewhere in Prague are closed from November 1 till March 31. (Parks, on the other hand, are open year-round, except in cases of extreme weather, such as floods which make the risk of trees falling a hazard due to loose roots.)

Tip: As I mentioned above, when touring Prague Castle, you can actually walk through all of the grounds and see most of the buildings from the outside without buying a ticket. (At least at the time of this writing, this is the case. But this could change as the new security measures continue to evolve – see "Security" below.) In fact, you can do this until late in the evenings (10:00 p.m. in the summer), which is actually quite a nice thing to do because it's not crowded at night, and in summer daylight lasts until 9:30 p.m. or so. You can also enter St. Vitus Cathedral at the western end without buying a ticket (see hours above). However, without a ticket you will not be able to venture very far into the building, nor can you visit the interiors of any other Castle sites. In my opinion, the Castle interiors are worth a visit – not only are they interesting, but some of them are also historically significant. But a tour of the Castle structures from the outside only is certainly worthwhile as well.

Duration

It will take you anywhere from two to three hours to complete the walk. Exactly how long it will take depends on such things as your pace, the weather, crowd levels, security lines, whether you visit one or more of the gardens, which starting point you choose, whether you walk up to Prague Castle from Malá Strana or take the tram up, etc.

Security

When I published my first book, "Prague Travel Tips: An American's Guide to Her Adopted City," I mentioned that there was talk of implementing security measures at Prague Castle, and when I wrote my first draft of this book, I said the same. Surprisingly, there was absolutely no security at the Castle or any of its sites, a fact that was both comforting and frightening at the same time, but also certainly in one sense a welcome break from the seemingly omnipresent security checks in the lives we live now. It was a relaxing "blast from the past."

Well, last summer, they finally did it – now you will have to go through security when you visit Prague Castle, and this is also, in a way, welcome (you will probably agree when you see the massive crowds packed into some of the small, enclosed spaces within the Castle complex).

However, there are a few issues that I'd like to point out:

• The security checks seem to have been implemented overnight with very little planning put into them. The authorities simply threw up security checkpoints from one day to the next, and ostensibly no thought or consideration was given to, and no accommodation whatsoever was made for, the resulting impact of implementing these measures, such as: the resulting lines and even larger crowds that this would create on the **unsecured** side of the security checks. This has resulted in some very inconvenient (and unsafe, quite frankly) situations, such as long lines of tourists forming in streets full of traffic, for one.

• As a result of the first point above, the number, location, and type of checks have changed several times since they were implemented. They could change again, **so anything I write here is subject to change, but this is the state of things as they stand as I take this book to press!** So, I apologize in advance if the checks are different from any information contained here, and I would love it if you would email me at krysti.brice@seznam.cz in case you find the security check (or anything else in this book) at odds with your experience.

• As of now, security checks involve passing through a metal detector and/or being waved with a wand and having your backpack and pockets searched. You might or might not receive a pat down.

• Do not expect the same level of curtesy, respect for personal space, communication about procedures, etc., as you would receive in the United States from TSA or in your home country if different from the USA (I know what you're thinking about TSA, but...). Those rules and norms do not apply here. And no thought whatsoever will be given to the gender of the person searching in relation to the person being searched. And you might get touched in some fairly private areas if the guard deems it necessary (or dare I say desirable?). This is not meant to put you off – just know what to expect/what is possible.

• Security checks are done at the entrance to the Royal Garden, at Prašný Most/Powder Bridge and at Hradčanské Náměstí. Also, if you approach the Castle from other locations not covered in this walk (the park in Jelení Příkop/Stag Moat or the Old Castle Steps), you will also face a security check.

• Based on my experience in conducting tours, the entrance at Hradčanské Náměstí consistently has the longest line, and it is **substantially** longer than the lines at any of the other entrances. That's because this is the official entrance to the Castle and is the location of the Castle Gates, and so that is where most tourists head when they want to visit.

• And not only is the line at Hradčanské Náměstí significantly longer than at the other checkpoints, it is usually enormous – hundreds of people – and it is like that at almost any time of day.

• By comparison, the lines at both the Powder Bridge (Prašný Most) and the Royal Garden are usually relatively small (the line at the Royal Garden is usually the smallest –

if it is the time of year during which it is open). And even if you see a rather large line at the Powder Bridge, it usually moves quickly. Just be aware that most large tour buses drop off their groups at the Powder Bridge entrance, and so if you arrive at the wrong moment, the wait could be long there as well. Most of the large tour buses arrive in the morning, between 9:00 and 10:30 a.m., so you might want to consider that in your planning.

So, I wish you luck with a short security line, and – again – this can change, but as I write this book, this is how it stands.

.

5 STARTING POINT 1 - THE ROYAL GARDEN AND THE ROYAL SUMMER PALACE (BELVEDERE)

The **Belvedere** (the **Royal Summer Palace** or **Queen Anne's Summer Palace**) is an exquisite Renaissance building dating to the middle of the 16th century. Emperor Ferdinand I summoned Italian architects to build it for his wife, Anne, as an expression of his love for her. Alas, she never saw the finished palace – she died giving birth to their fifteenth (yes, **fifteenth!**) child. But the building that has outlived both Anne and her husband is a delectable example of the Renaissance architectural style.

The current roof of the Belvedere was done by the court architect to Ferdinand, Bonifaz Wohlmut, and was completed in 1563. Shaped like a ship's hull, it was a geometrical, architectural, and engineering marvel at the time it was built. The lightness created by the palace's arches and the relative narrowness of the Ionic columns supporting them gives an airiness and delicacy to the structure that is ahead of its time. This was the first Renaissance structure in Gothic Prague and reportedly was the first Renaissance building north of the Alps. The stucco work in the frieze is also notable for how fine and intricate it is. It was created by Italian artisans also brought to Prague by Ferdinand.

The Belvedere and the Singing Fountain

The so-called **"Singing" Fountain** just in front of the Belvedere is a metallurgical marvel. This bronze work was cast by a master bell founder in 1564. The fall of water from the fountain onto the basin produces a ringing sound from whence it gets its name. But you'll have to stick your head up under it (and maybe get a little wet) to hear the fountain "sing."

When facing the Belvedere with the Singing Fountain at your back, walk to your right to the edge of the garden for some wonderful views of Prague and the Castle's fortifications across the former moat, with a glimpse of the fig garden below you.

Now turn until the Belvedere is at your back with the Castle on your left and walk along the garden path. Along the way, take note of the various trees and shrubs planted in the garden, most of which are marked with signs in both Czech and English indicating their species. The **Royal Garden** was originally laid out in 1534 in the Italian style of garden and was converted to the French Baroque style in the early 18th century. Later that century, the garden was devastated by the Prussians, and in the 19th century it was redone in the English style.

Continuing in the same direction, the next building you'll come to is the **New Orangery (Oranžerie)** on your left (it is actually set back a little from and below the path on which you're walking), on the castle side of the garden. Look for a path that leads to a small terrace overlooking both the Orangery and the former moat. The terrace also offers an exquisite view of the Castle and of St. Vitus Cathedral in particular.

Note: In 2016, the garden's shrubbery along the moat (south) side of the garden was cut back significantly, meaning that now you can get fantastic views of the northern side of St. Vitus Cathedral throughout the garden. This is a good thing, since Maria Theresa's edifice (you'll read more about that later) on the south side of the castle complex blocks much of the cathedral when viewed from Old Town or the Lesser Quarter (Malá Strana).

The New Orangery was designed by renowned Czech architect Eva Jiřičná. In 1968, Jiřičná emigrated from former Czechoslovakia to the U.K., where she built quite a career for herself and earned many commissions for things like a new entrance and reception for the Victoria & Albert Museum and new shopping halls for Harrods in London, among others. When the Berlin wall came down, she returned to her native Prague, where she quickly got to work on Prague's first designer hotel, the Josef, and later on another sleek Prague hotel, the Maximillian.

The New Orangery

In the 1990s, the city of Prague commissioned her to design a new orangery to replace the old one in the Royal Garden. It was completed in 1998 and is the newest structure at the Castle. The steel and glass construction is typical of Jiřícná's work, so she was a perfect candidate to build a glasshouse (check out the lobby of Hotel Josef in Old Town for a comparison). Her New Orangery is a great new addition to the Castle, Prague's oldest quarter.

Return to the path on the south side of the garden, and as you continue in the same direction (with the Belvedere at your back), the next structure you'll come to is the **Míčovna** (the **Ball Game Hall** or **Ball Hall**) on the left. Designed by Bonifaz Wohlmut and built in the 1560s, the name describes the place well – the Míčovna was a precursor to a racquetball club or an indoor tennis court (except that this one is a lot more upscale than its modern-day descendants).

The Ball Hall or Míčovna

The Hapsburgs built this recreational center in the 16th century, complete with extremely fine sgraffito work that was a hallmark of Renaissance decoration. Take a look at the inscriptions alongside each column toward their tops, and you'll notice images representing allegories of the sciences, virtues and elements, such as "prudence" and "charity." When you find the word "justice," look just to the right of the column to **its** right, and you'll find a hammer and sickle in the sgraffito that the Communists snuck in.

Note: Sgraffito comes from the Latin word meaning "to scratch." It is created by mixing one color of mortar, applying it to a surface and letting it dry. Then a second layer of mortar in a contrasting color is applied, and before it dries, a design is stenciled onto it and the top (wet) layer is pulled, or scratched, away with special tools. Sgraffito is also where we get the word "graffiti."

Detail of the Mičovna's sgraffito

Continue along the path in the same direction, making your way toward the iron gates that open onto **U Prašného Mostu Street,** stopping along the way for the photo-ops of St. Vitus on your left (some of the best views of the cathedral will be just before you exit through the gates).

When you reach the iron gates and exit onto U Prašného Mostu, look to your right and you'll notice a long, narrow building on the opposite side of the street. This is the **Prague Castle Riding School (Jízdárna Pražského Hradu).**

Next we will merge with **Starting Point 2**.

6 STARTING POINT 2 – PRAGUE CASTLE RIDING SCHOOL ON U PRAŠNÉHO MOSTU STREET

Starting Point 2 picks up here. Those who began the walk at Starting Point 2 will arrive at this spot after passing through security. The building you passed on your right is the **Prague Castle Riding School (Jízdárna Pražského Hradu).**

Built in the late 17th century (1694-95), this Baroque building has been used for art exhibitions (apparently it is the largest exhibition space in Prague) since the mid-twentieth century. Check to see what's on in case you're interested. But even if you're not, this venue has a gift shop, a café (both indoors and on an outdoor terrace in an inner courtyard in warmer months), an ATM ("bankomat") and a restroom inside (enter to the left of the main exhibition entrance). The restroom requires coins, but I believe this one has a machine that will change your bills for you.

View of the Prague Castle Riding School from the Powder
Bridge

Now head toward the Castle entrance which is on the
other side of the **Powder Bridge (Prašný Most)** that
crosses the former **Stag Moat (Jelení Příkop).** The moat
has now been turned into a park and footpath. It makes
for a nice walk in the woods while still being in the city
(closed in the winter months, so check listings).

The bridge affords more great views of St. Vitus and
the moat, as well as views of the 15th-century Castle
fortifications by architect Benedikt Ried (see **Vladislav
Hall** in Chapter 8). As you approach the castle, you'll see
some of the castle guards in their dress uniforms on either
side of the entrance. This spot rather than the main gate
offers better photo ops as it's usually less crowded (and the
security check at the main entrance might mean that no
photo op will exist there by the time you visit).

View of the Stag Moat from the Powder Bridge

View of the Powder Tower (Mihulka), part of the Castle
fortifications, from the Powder Bridge

If you like the guards' snazzy uniforms, it's no surprise.
When playwright and former dissident Václav Havel was
first elected president in 1989 (the first democratically-
elected president of former Czechoslovakia in 41 years), he
noticed, among (many) other things, how drab the green
communist uniforms of the guards at his new home were.
So, he called up a friend of his who happened to be the

costume designer for the movie "Amadeus" and had him design new uniforms for the Prague Castle Guard. What you see is the result.

Prague Castle Guards

Note: The movie "Amadeus" was filmed almost entirely in Prague (in the last decade of Communist rule). The film's Czech-born director, Miloš Forman, needed a place that looked like 18th-century Vienna, and in in Prague he found a film set in waiting. Not only is "Amadeus" a great film, but it also provides a glimpse of Prague as it once looked before all of the post-communist renovations began. But even then, the city's beauty and history were evident.

After you've taken your photos, continue into the Castle grounds via the passage way on the left (be aware that the center route between the two guards is an active roadway for presidential office staff, so it's best to take the passageway on the left). **While inside the passageway you'll see a sign for an information office on the left.**

You can **buy tickets to the Castle sites here** (there's usually a shorter line at this office than in the main office in the courtyard you're about to enter) **or at the ticket office which is located just to the right after you enter the large expanse of courtyard** (officially called the **Second Courtyard**) which opens up on the other end of the passageway.

Entering the Second Courtyard from the Powder Bridge

When facing the ticket office/information center in the Second Courtyard, you'll find a small passageway to the left of it. In it is an exposed area behind a glass wall on the right. These are some of the oldest remnants of the original settlement at Prague Castle. These ruins of the **Church of the Virgin Mary** date to the 9th century.

The ticket office in the Second Courtyard

Opening revealing ruins of the Church of the Virgin Mary

Continue through the passageway and into an open space. On the right-hand side you'll see a large terrace with sleek circular stairs. This modern touch in the form of a neo-Classical pavilion called the **Garden on the Bastion (Na Baště)** was added by the architect Rottmayer who built on the work of Josip Plečnik, whom you'll learn about later.

Staircase at the Garden on the Bastion

Stop here, turn back around and return to the **Second Courtyard** (otherwise, if you exit the gates in front of you, you will have to go through security again, and, in fact, I believe it's now forbidden to exit here because of security). When you reach the Second Courtyard again, turn right and walk along the inner wall on your right. When you come to a series of archways on the right, turn and walk under them and through to the **First Courtyard.** But, as with the exit near the Church of the Virgin Mary, **do not exit the gates flanked by the battling Baroque giants** that you are now viewing from their rear (with a view of their rears). You would have to go through security again.

Now that you are in the **First Courtyard,** you will have to be satisfied with reading about the sites of **Hradčanské Náměstí** while viewing them through the iron fence of this courtyard (and please forgive the repetition later where I will guide people from **Starting Point 3** past the Church of the Virgin Mary, to the ticket office, etc.).

OR

Skip to Chapter 8 where **Starting Points 1 and 2** resume and merge with the route from **Starting Point 3**. If you have time later, you could return to **Hradčanské Náměstí** and its description in this book and see its sites up close after you finish the walk.

7 STARTING POINT 3 – HRADČANSKÉ NÁMĚSTÍ

After either walking up Nerudova Street from the Malá Strana or down Loretánská Street from the Pohořelec tram stop, you will end up at this expansive square in front of the battling giants at the Castle Gate. This is where your walk begins.

Battling Giants at the Prague Castle Gates

This is **Hradčanské Náměstí (Castle Square),** and in addition to being lined with rather large palaces, it also affords **fantastic views** of Prague off to the right of the giants as you face them. Walk over to the wall where you'll see a lookout telescope (and probably lots of people taking pictures of the view as well as selfies). From this spot you'll be looking out over the terra cotta rooftops of the small houses located on Malá Strana's tiny lanes.

At this point you'll also notice a Starbucks occupying the structure built into the wall you're now looking over. Fortunately, Starbucks did a very good job of making this particular location as inconspicuous as possible. But make no mistake, this outlet is like no other Starbucks in the world, I would guess. Almost every seat has a view like the one you're taking in now, and there is also ample outdoor seating on the large terrace below that gives one the feeling of sharing a cup of coffee in a friend's garden (open in warmer months only).

Starbucks with stunning views of Malá Strana

After taking in the views and perhaps having a drink, turn back around and return to the space in front of the gates. As you're walking back uphill, you'll see a statue on your left marked with the letters "TGM." This is **Tomáš Garrigue Masaryk,** the first president of the (then) new democracy of the newly-created country of Czechoslovakia. Masaryk's wife was American, and her maiden name was Garrigue, which her husband took as an additional name when they married; hence the initials "TGM."

Statue of Tomáš Garrigue Masaryk

Behind Masaryk is the **Salm Palace** from 1810, and next to it is the sgraffito-covered **Schwarzenberg Palace.** If the nobility of the Hapsburg Empire wanted to build their palaces in the Malá Strana in order to be close to the seat of power at Prague Castle, then the palaces on Hradčanské Náměstí belonged to the real bigwigs. The size and grandeur of these structures reflects this fact. Many of the palaces on Hradčanské Náměstí, like the Salm and Schwarzenberg palaces, now belong to the **National Gallery in Prague,** and most of them contain a permanent exhibition of a particular genre of art, while some of them also host temporary exhibitions.

The Schwarzenberg Palace

The Schwarzenberg Palace is one of the most well-preserved (and one of the few) Renaissance palaces in Prague. It is covered in rich sgraffito decoration and was built by the Lobkowicz family in the 16th century, after the great fire of 1541. After passing through several families' hands, it was acquired by the Schwarzenberg family in 1719. It now houses the National Gallery's Bohemian Baroque art collection.

On the opposite side of the square is the beautiful white **Archbishop's Palace (Arcibiskupcý Palác).** Ferdinand I commissioned this magnificent building in the late 16th century, and it has been the seat of Prague's archbishop ever since. It was originally designed in the Renaissance style. Later it was rebuilt in the Baroque and finally in the Rococo style (in the 1760s) that you see now.

The Archbishop's Palace

Now return to the **Battling Giants.** These are 20th century copies of the originals which were done in the 1760s by **Ignác Platzer.** Platzer also decorated the façade of the Archbishop's Palace and did the enormous statues of saints John the Baptist and John the Evangelist in Malá Strana's **St. Nicholas Church,** whose dome dominates the view of the Malá Strana you just took in when surveying the views of Prague.

The giants are flanked by the Czech lion and the Moravian eagle, which were also done by Platzer. Below the gates stand more members of the **Castle Guard,** and if you're here at noon, you'll have the opportunity to see the changing of the guard ceremony (though other, less elaborate, guard changings happen at all of the Castle's gates on the hour until 8:00 p.m. in the summer and until 6:00 p.m. in the winter).

The Castle Guard

Note: The site of the changing of the guard might have moved, most likely to the Third Courtyard, due to the new security measures.

If you like the guards' snazzy uniforms, it's no surprise. When playwright and former dissident Václav Havel was first elected president in 1989 (the first democratically-elected president of former Czechoslovakia in 41 years), he noticed, among (many) other things, how drab the green communist uniforms of the guards at his new home were. So, he called up a friend of his who happened to be the costume designer for the movie "Amadeus" and had him design new uniforms for the Prague Castle Guard. What you see is the result.

Note: The movie "Amadeus" was filmed almost entirely in Prague (in the last decade of Communist rule). The film's Czech-born director, Miloš Forman, needed a place that looked like 18th-century Vienna, and in in Prague he found a film set in waiting. Not only is "Amadeus" a great film, but it also provides a glimpse of Prague as it once looked before all of the post-communist renovations began. But even then, the city's beauty and history were evident.

Now you will have to pass through security at the smaller gates to the left of these main Castle Gates. You should have no trouble spotting the line. Once you clear security, you'll find yourself in a small courtyard with a large terrace with sleek circular stairs on the left. This modern touch in the form of a neo-Classical pavilion called the Garden on the Bastion (Na Baště) was added by the architect Rottmayer who built on the work of Josip Plečnik, whom you'll learn about later.

Stairs leading to the Garden on the Bastion

Follow the crowds into the passageway in front of you with the security check at your back.

Opening revealing ruins of the Church of the Virgin Mary

In the passageway is an exposed area behind a glass wall on the left. These are some of the oldest remnants of the original settlement at Prague Castle. These ruins of the **Church of the Virgin Mary** date to the 9th century.

Now continue in the same direction into the large expanse of courtyard (officially called the **Second Courtyard**) on the other end of the passageway. **Immediately to your left you'll see an information sign that marks a ticket office where you can buy tickets to the Castle sites.**

Ticket office in the Second Courtyard

When you exit the ticket office, turn right, and move along the inner wall of the Second Courtyard that divides it from the First Courtyard. When you come to a series of archways on the right, turn and walk under them and through to the **First Courtyard.**

Once you are in the First Courtyard, **do not exit the gates flanked by the battling Baroque giants** that you are now viewing from their rear (with a view of their rears). You would again have to go through security.

8 THE FIRST COURTYARD – ALL STARTING POINTS

Starting Points 1 and 2 resume here – If you began the walk at either **Starting Point 1 or Starting Point 2,** you should have reached this point in the **First Courtyard** after seeing the Church of the Virgin Mary and purchasing your tickets.

At this point, all three Starting Points are in the same place.

Having passed through the arches leading to the **First Courtyard,** turn around 180 degrees and face the passageway through which you just came. In front of you will be the **Matthias Gate.** On each side of the gate are two giant flagpoles. These are examples of several modern additions to the Castle which were done in the 1920s by Slovenian architect **Josip Plečnik.** Plečnik was hired by President Masaryk to make "modernizations" to Prague Castle, with the aim of creating "architecture for a new democracy." Plečnik's unmistakable touch can be seen throughout Prague Castle, and his work makes up some of my favorite features at the site. The flagpoles, like most of

Plečnik's work, look ahead of their time (as well as looking like the masts of ships). And though they look rather new at the moment due to a recent refinishing, they are the originals. The flagpoles are made of fir trees from the mountain ranges of the Czech Republic's border regions.

One of Plečnik's flagpoles

The **Matthias Gate** dates to the beginning of the 17th

century and once stood alone at the Castle's entrance. This structure, made of Meissen sandstone, is mainly Mannerist in style with a hint of Baroque – one of the earliest touches of Baroque in Prague, in fact, and the city's first secular Baroque structure. The Matthias Gate is credited to the Italian architect Filippi, but some dispute this. The shields on this triumphal arch are those of the lands ruled by the Hapsburgs at the time it was erected.

The Matthias Gate

The Matthias Gate is set into the palatial building that surrounds it. This neo-Classical-looking edifice houses the former throne room and royal private apartments, as well as the current offices and private apartments of the Czech president and the offices of the president's administration. Its construction was commissioned in the mid-18th century by Hapsburg Empress Maria Theresa who had it designed by her architect, Nicolo Picassi. Her motivation was a desire to give Prague Castle a uniform look resembling a Viennese palace. As a result, Prague Castle has the appearance of being one large structure when viewed from the south side, but an exploration of the 1,100-year history and architecture of the nexus of buildings within the Castle complex belies the uniform appearance of the façade.

As was mentioned earlier, Prague Castle was actually a fortress and a "town" encompassing most of the aspects of a medieval community and more. And Maria Theresa's illusion is further revealed when you consider that her grand edifice is located only on the "front" of the Castle – the south side which is visible from the town below. She didn't bother with the back (the northern side). This addition was built on top of the old Castle walls.

Now pass back through the Matthias Gate and stop just under the arches of Picassi's palace and look to the right. Through the glass in the doors you can get a peek at Picassi's late Rococo interior style. Now turn to the left and look at the interior on the other side by Plečnik. This is known as the Hall of Columns, and with its Doric columns is typical of Plečnik's work.

Take note of the flat ceiling, the two levels of simple columns, with the upper level giving the impression of a clerestory. To me, Plecnik's work looks both ancient and modern at the same time. Many of his structures seem to have a Minoan feel, and this interior is also reminiscent of the interior of Plecnik's Kostel Nejsvětějšho Srdce Páně (Church of the Sacred Heart) at Náměstí Jiřího z Poděbrad in the Vinohrady neighborhood.

Palace interior by Picassi

Plečnik's Hall of Columns

From here continue out of the archway and into the Second Courtyard. Immediately ahead of you and slightly to the left you'll see a majestic view of the spires of **St. Vitus Cathedral ("St. Vitus" or "the Cathedral")** rising above another section of Picassi's palace. On the right on the opposite side of the courtyard from where you are standing is the **Chapel of the Holy Rood,** also by Picassi, and on the left of the courtyard is a late 17th-century

Baroque fountain.

Note: The chapel, which was designed by Picassi but built by Anselmo Lurago in the 1750s, holds the Treasury of St. Vitus, and is one of the richest cathedral treasuries in Central Europe. Entry to the treasury is not included in the short visit ticket which is covered by this walk. You can buy a separate ticket for the Treasury's exhibition at the ticket office.

The Chapel of the Holy Rood

Now we'll move on to **St. Vitus Cathedral.** The original St. Vitus church was a Romanesque rotunda founded in the 10th century by St. Wenceslas, whose glorious chapel you'll see inside the present-day Cathedral. Duke (now Saint) Wenceslas had the first church built in order to house a holy relic: the shoulder of St. Vitus which was given to him by Emperor Henry the Fowler. From that point on, Vitus has been a patron saint of Bohemia.

St. Wenceslas chose the highest point in the Castle on

which to place the Church, and all of the subsequent versions of St. Vitus – a 70-meter long Romanesque basilica with a center nave and two side aisles from the 11th century, commissioned by Prince Spytihněv, and the Gothic Cathedral you are about to tour – have stood on the same spot. It was Charles IV, King and Emperor, who commissioned the Gothic Cathedral, and in doing so intended to make Prague Castle and St. Vitus the center of his reign and Czech statehood. It also symbolized Prague's being elevated to an archbishopric from a bishopric.

Note: Technically, in order to be called a cathedral, a church must meet one of two requirements: 1) It must be either the seat of a bishop or of an archbishop, and/or 2) it must have radiating chapels, that is chapels that radiate around the altar with a space between the row of chapels and the altar creating an aisle through which you can walk behind the altar.

Awning above the entrance to the President's offices by Plečnik

In the Cathedral are the graves of King Charles' forebears, including St. Wenceslas, who was buried in the original rotunda. When Charles had the Cathedral built, he instructed his architect, Peter Parler, to arrange the design around the original burial place of St. Wenceslas, who was given a special place of honor in his chapel mentioned above.

Now cross the courtyard diagonally to your left (in a northeasterly direction toward the cathedral spires, passing the fountain on your left), taking note of **Plečnik's copper awning and golden griffin-like creature** on the eastern side of the courtyard. Enter one of the two passageways that lead to St. Vitus Cathedral. When you come out of the passageway, you'll be directly in front of the church's impressive façade.

Note: **Be careful when you exit here. For one thing, cars occasionally pass through this passageway, so be on the lookout. And for another, the spot right in front of St. Vitus is a prime pickpocket target area.** The reasons why will become immediately apparent once you get there. It is a small space where huge crowds not only funnel through a bottleneck created by the passageways, but then everyone stops in the small space between the passageways and the front of the church and stares upwards at the beautiful façade taking photos. With so many people crowded into a small area with their attention focused on the soaring Cathedral, and with it being difficult to move, it's a field day if someone wants to lift a wallet. **My advice is to move immediately to the right or to the left once you exit the passageway and then back up to the wall.** It will be less crowded, and no one can sneak up from behind you. Then you can marvel at the Cathedral in peace.

The façade of St. Vitus Cathedral

Though St. Vitus was begun in the 14th century, the façade you're now facing is actually from the 20th century. Closer inspection will make this evident. Take note of the stones making up this, the western end of the Cathedral. They are all uniform in shape and size. The mortar between the joints is also quite thin as well as rather exact.

Precisely-cut and regularly-sized stones in the newer, 20th-century façade of St. Vitus

A closer look at the delicate carving, especially that of the tympanum (the triangular space above the door), reveals quite "modern" statuary done most likely with the help of machines. If you've already seen the 14th-century tympanum at the Týn Church on Old Town square, you will be able to discern a big difference between the two.

The tympanum above the western entrance of St. Vitus
Cathedral

Like many churches in Bohemia, the construction of St.
Vitus was stopped during the Hussite Wars which began in
the early 15th century. In some cases, churches were
totally ransacked, and many of those were never rebuilt.
In other cases, a temporary wall went up at the farthest
point where construction had reached, and the temporary
wall might have remained for centuries. Sometimes this
end point was later made into a permanent wall, as was the
case for St. Barbora's Cathedral in Kutná Hora, for
example.

**In the case of St. Vitus, however, nearly five
centuries after a temporary wall went up, a decision
was undertaken to complete the church in the
originally conceived proportions.** The entire western
end of the church was completed in the late 19th and early
20th centuries, staying very true to the original design and
style. The resulting appearance gives a quite seamless
impression of a glorious medieval Gothic cathedral that,

upon closer inspection, reveals the very "new" construction of the western end. On the other hand, this also offers an opportunity to compare the old and the new, the different building techniques and materials, and the different styles, some of which were the result of the progression of technology and some of which were not.

In my opinion, the "old" part of St. Vitus is much more beautiful, interesting and impressive than the "new" part. The "new" part is **construction,** built according to plan using machines (and man). The "old" part is **art** – part tapestry of hand-cut and -carved stone and part mosaic, part fortress and part painting. **Before entering the church,** let's compare and contrast the old and new from the exterior of St. Vitus's and you'll begin to see what I mean.

From the front of the church, walk to the left of it and continue along the (northern) side of the Cathedral toward the transept. Soon you'll notice several staircases in front of the buildings on the left side of the lane (Vikářská), and opposite the northern side of the church. Continue until you reach the third staircase on your left, and stop. Here you will be able to see the first 14th-century column in the eastern end of the Cathedral and the difference between the old and new parts of the structure.

King Charles IV, who is considered the greatest king to ever rule Bohemia (he ruled from 1346 to 1378), grew up and was educated in France, and it was in France that he fell in love with the Gothic style. So, when he ascended to the Bohemian throne, he punctuated his rule with monuments done in a style that became known as "International Gothic." St. Vitus is the pinnacle of this Gothic era in Prague: Charles' aim in building it was to give Prague and his kingdom a central focal point and to give a monument to himself for posterity. He seems to have succeeded.

Stairway on Vikářská from which to view the first older
columns of the northern side of St. Vitus

Because Charles wanted a French-style Gothic cathedral,
he initially hired a French architect, **Matthias of Arras,** to
build it. But Matthias died not long after the project was
begun (Matthias built eight chapels in the eastern end).
Charles then called on **Peter Parler,** the descendant of a

German stone-cutting family from Swabia (Parler built the remaining chapels radiating around the choir where the high alter stands, the triforium and the roof over the choir). Parler, a talented builder and stone carver who had recently worked on the great cathedral in Cologne, changed Arras's plans from a French style to a more German one, with added height, and in doing so turned St. Vitus into his masterpiece. At the same time, he ushered in a period in which Prague became the most significant center of Gothic architecture in Europe. Both architects are buried in the Cathedral in one of the chapels in the eastern end. This was a rare honor for the day.

KRYSTI BRICE

Older 14th-century part of northern wall of St. Vitus

One of the first things you might notice is that the walls, columns and buttresses of the older part look as if they are made up of a patchwork of stones (this is in contrast to the precisely-cut, evenly-spaced, uniformly-sized stones that we saw at the western end and in the first part of the wall you've just walked along). The stones in the older part, having been cut by hand and therefore necessarily more closely conforming to their original natural size and shape, are a mishmash of colors, sizes – and shapes. The mortar between them is thick and

68

somewhat unruly, adding to the patchwork, almost "mosaic" effect.

Come back to the front (western end) of the church and enter it.

Tip: Sometimes the lines to get into the Cathedral are **enormous**, and that is usually in the mornings (between 9:00 and 11:00 a.m.). The reasons for this are numerous: 1) the Cathedral is the only part of the Castle whose interior can be visited free of charge, so all the large "budget" tour companies take advantage of this fact and take their customers on a quick walk through the Castle grounds and into the Cathedral without having to purchase a ticket; 2) most tourists, and especially the large tour groups, visit the Castle in the morning; 3) if it is raining, all those non-ticketholders run to the Cathedral for cover, as it is the only building they can enter without a ticket, and 4) given the large crowds and the new security-consciousness at the Castle, the authorities have now taken to enacting crowd-control in St. Vitus (which is actually quite welcome). If the lines are excessively long when you get ready to enter, consider visiting one of the other sites on your ticket (such as the Old Royal Palace or St. George's Basilica) first, and then return to the Cathedral later. This usually avoids the problem, as you will most likely find that the lines have magically disappeared as the large groups have moved on to their next destination.

Once inside St. Vitus, but before venturing very far, just stand at the back looking east down the nave toward the high altar at the other end. From this point, take in the magnificence of the structure – its width (60 m/197 ft), length (124 m/407 ft) and height (33 m/108 ft). The size and proportions combine to stunning effect: the soaring height, the staggering length, the colorful glow of the stained glass, and – if you're lucky enough to be there on a sunny day and at the right time in the afternoon when the sun is shining through the rose window above you on the western end – the dance of color on the large columns at the rear combine into an almost mystical experience (but for the crowds armed with smartphones in selfie sticks).

The nave of St. Vitus

And yet, even from here, taking in the overall effect of the view of the Cathedral from its 14th-century eastern end to the 20th-century western end where you are now standing, the contrast between old and new can be seen if you look closely. Notice that the nave in the older, farther end, softly illuminated with golden light, is slightly narrower than in the newer end. And though it might be a little harder to discern from here, the distance between the columns on each side of nave is a bit greater in the newer end than in the older, and, as a result, the points at the tops of the arches in the newer end are less acute. In my view, the sharpness of the points of the arches in Peter Parler's work adds to its beauty and drama.

As with the outside, the stones in the western end where you're standing now are precisely cut with very little mortar between them. Looking down the aisle toward the eastern end, notice the first large arch over the nave just past the transept. Immediately you can discern that the stones making it up are smaller, irregularly-cut and -sized and have more mortar between them than those in the newer part (the mortar between the stones in the first large arch over the older part of the nave almost looks like thick painted white stripes). The colors of the stones in the older arch vary, as well, repeating the "mosaic" effect visible on the building's exterior.

Turnstiles leading to the older part of the Cathedral

The first three chapels on each side in the western end are from the 20th century, as are their stained glass windows. When you're ready, move to the left (northern) aisle and scan your ticket at the turnstiles to enter the parts of the Cathedral that are restricted to ticketholders (which are the really interesting bits). You're now in the northern aisle, and the third chapel that you come to on the left as you walk toward the older, eastern end of the Cathedral is the **New Archbishop's Chapel.**

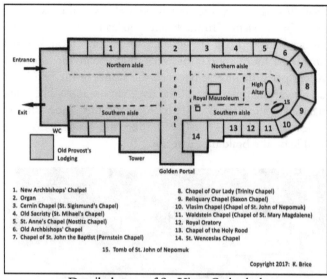

Detailed map of St. Vitus Cathedral

This chapel is significant for a couple of reasons. One is its stained glass window depicting tales from the lives of Saints Cyril and Methodius, Macedonian monks who brought religion to the Slavic peoples in the 9th century, along with the alphabet the monks had devised in order to translate the Bible into the Old Slavonic language from Greek (today it is known as the Cyrillic alphabet). You might recognize from the style that this window is the work of artist **Alfons Mucha,** the renowned Czech Art Nouveau painter known for, among other things, the paintings of advertisements he created for French biscuit maker Lefevre-Utile.

Alfons Mucha's Window in the New Archbishop's Chapel

The other reason for this chapel's significance is the fact that **Archbishop František Tomášek,** the 34th archbishop of Prague who served during communist times, is buried here. Tomášek was mocked by the communist regime as a "general without an army." But the bishop had the last laugh. He outlived the regime and witnessed its demise and fall in 1989. His funeral was held here in St. Vitus in 1992, and in attendance were Czech President Vaclav Havel and Polish President Lech Walesa. Sometimes justice is sweet.

Tip: If you're a fan of Mucha, or just of Art Nouveau, the Mucha Museum on Panská Street near Wenceslas Square is worth a visit.

Moving further along, passing a neo-Gothic stairwell on your left, you'll come to a new addition in the aisle, also on the left just before the transept – a wooden crucifix dating to 1899 by **František Bílek,** a renowned Czech sculptor whose work often had religious themes.

Tip: Another of Bílek's works, a bronze statue of Moses, is located in Prague's Jewish Quarter. The original Moses was destroyed by the Nazis. However, though the artist was deceased at that point, some of his former students recast the present statue from Bílek's mold. You will pass Bílek's Moses statue on my Jewish Quarter Walk. Also, if you took the tram up from the Malá Strana on your way to the Castle, you would have passed Bílek's unusual villa which he designed for himself just before reaching the Kralovský Letohradek stop. The villa can be visited daily except Mondays. Check listings for the Prague City Gallery at www.ghmp.cz/villa-bilek.

After taking a few steps more until you reach the transept, you'll now be at the part of the church that gets really interesting. And here at the point where the transept crosses the center aisle, you're in a perfect spot to observe the "old" part of the church done by master architect Peter Parler which lies to the east.

Immediately you'll be struck by the beauty of his design and the artistic look of the structure. Here the stones, with their varying shapes, sizes and colors, really look like a hand-wrought mosaic. The soft golden tint of the upper windows above the high altar adds a surreal glow to this part of the Cathedral, and the rougher cut of the stones when compared to the newer part have an earthiness and simplicity to their look despite the precision that emerges when viewing them as a whole. And while the builders who completed the western end in the 20th century remained true to Parler's original style and design, they could not mimic the artistry of the hand-cut stonework that strikes the eye when looking at the overall effect of the older construction.

The 14ᵗʰ-century choir in the eastern end of St. Vitus

Take your time comparing the two parts and enjoying the beauty before you, including the largest window in St. Vitus over the south entrance on the opposite side of the transept from where you are. It depicts the Last Judgment and is the work of **Max Švabinský,** a Czech painter and graphic artist born in 1873. This window, completed in 1934, contains 40,000 pieces of glass.

On the opposite (northern) side of the transept is the organ gallery done by Bonifaz Wohlmut in the mid-16th century. The organ is 18th-century Baroque and has 6,500 pipes. The Cathedral will get a new organ soon (it is due to be played for the first time in October 2019, according to an article in the *Prague Daily Monitor*).

Moving east in the northern aisle, on the left you'll see the **Černín Chapel** (St. Sigismund Chapel). The large Baroque altar was designed by the architect František Kaňka, whom you'll learn more about when you visit St. George's Basilica. Both the Černín Chapel and the following one (see map), known as the **Old Sacristy** (or

St. Michael's Chapel), were the work of Peter Parler. Note the fine vaulting by Parler in the Old Sacristy.

Window by Max Švabinský on the southern end of the transept

As you continue down the left (northern) aisle toward the altar, on the right in the middle of the choir is the white marble **Royal Mausoleum (also called the Hapsburg Mausoleum).** Depicted sleeping atop it in full regalia are Emperor Ferdinand I, his wife, Anne, and their son, Emperor Maximillian II. They were all buried here after being brought to Prague from Vienna in a huge funeral procession in the late 16th century. The sarcophagus was carved from Austrian marble by a Dutch sculptor, Alexander Collin, and is enclosed in an original Renaissance grille.

Note: This work of art is one of the few made of marble in the former Bohemian kingdom. That's because the Czech Republic has no marble to be quarried, so the few marble structures you'll find here were imported from elsewhere. One result of this lack of marble was that Prague's stucco artists became some of the best in the world at their craft, which you will notice as you walk through Prague's historic streets.

The Hapsburg Mausoleum in the center of the choir of St. Vitus, surrounded by an iron grille

Take a few more steps along the northern aisle in an easterly direction and look to the opposite (southern) aisle on the other side of the church. Though you'll get an up-close look in a few minutes when you circle around to the other side of the nave, the vantage point from here on the opposite side offers a better perspective of the **Royal Oratory** designed by court architect Benedikt Ried for Vladislav II of Hungary in the late 15th century. (Vladislav was also known as Vladislav II and Vladislav Jagellonský in Czech. He was a Polish king who gained control of Bohemia and Hungary through marriage and ruled from 1471 to 1516.)

Peter Parler was the first architect on continental Europe to take Gothic vaulting beyond function and added more form. The webbing of ribs in the vaults above the choir/high altar of St. Vitus is a prime example.

Previously, a simple "cross vault" of one rib crossing another was all that could be found in the ceilings of Gothic structures. Here, Parler employs what came to be known as the "net" vault, as the ribbing looks like a net.

Following in the footsteps of Peter Parler, Ried took Parler's expressive work and ingenuity a step further, as you'll also see in Vladislav Hall of the Old Royal Palace. In that structure, Ried's work began to borrow on nature motifs, but the Oratory that you're observing now is even more directly influenced by nature with its decorations and vault carved in the shape of tree branches. It is so realistic-looking that you would think it's made from wood, but these decorations are actually carved out of stone.

Continuing in the same direction, next you'll come to a huge oak relief panel on the right side of the northern aisle in which you're standing depicting the **flight of the army of Frederick of the Palatinate** in 1620, after his defeat at the Battle of White Mountain. The remarkable things about this piece of artwork, besides the artistry itself and its size, are 1) the fact that it has survived in one piece undamaged for four centuries (it was done before 1630), and 2) the fact that, other than the addition of some Baroque buildings and façades, especially in the Malá Strana, Prague today looks pretty much as it appears in this relief. Look carefully and you'll be able to identify several Prague landmarks that you might already have visited, such as the Týn Church on the far left of the panel, the Old Town Hall not far from it to the right, and, of course, the Charles Bridge and Old Town Bridge Tower. This remarkable work was carved by Kaspar Bechteler (note that the plaque says that it was carved "before 1630," but some sources name the year precisely as 1623).

Opposite the oak relief is the **St. Anne's Chapel** (or

the Nostitz Chapel) and next to it as you continue east is the **Old Archbishop's Chapel.** Opposite it is a bronze statue of a kneeling cardinal. This image of **Bedřich Schwarzenberg** from 1895 was done by Czech sculptor Josef Václav Myslbek.

After the Old Archbishop's Chapel comes the **Chapel of St. John the Baptist** (or the Pernstein Chapel), and at the apex of the Cathedral is the **Chapel of our Lady** (also known as the Chapel of the Holy Trinity or the Imperial Chapel). It contains the tombs of Břetislav I and Spytihněv II, both of whom ruled in the 11th century. The rulers' tombs, however, are from the workshop of Peter Parler and are from the 14th century.

Opposite this chapel, just behind the high altar, is the **Tomb of St. Vitus.** But, alas, the Cathedral's namesake is outdone by the next grand tomb. Continuing around the curve of the aisle and the radiating chapels, you'll reach one of the most incredible sites in St. Vitus: the **Tomb of St. John of Nepomuk.** You can't miss it because it is so spectacular (either that, or because there will likely be a huge crowd gathered around it). **My advice is to take time to read this description before venturing there, as it will be too crowded and busy to read in peace once you reach it.**

John had been martyred when King Wenceslas IV, Charles' son, had him thrown off of the Charles Bridge and into the Vltava River for refusing to tell the king what his wife had told John in confession. This happened back in the late 14th century, but it was not until the early 18th century that John became Saint John when he was canonized in 1729. As part of their attempt to re-Catholicize the Czech population following victory in the Thirty Years' War, the Hapsburgs employed many tactics, such as the use of Baroque architecture (and when that didn't work, forced conversion, threat of exile and worse). The canonization of John was an attempt by the Hapsburgs to show their reverence for good Czech Catholics who had sacrificed for the Church.

Once John had been decided upon as the Czech martyr around whom to build a cult, his remains were exhumed, and a gathered expert committee examined his skull and declared that his tongue (the relevant, reverent organ that had refused to function when Wenceslas requested him to break his holy vow) was still alive. Later, another committee swore that John's tongue was not only alive but still growing! With two miracles documented, John was made a saint.

To show their reverence for St. John, the Hapsburgs moved his remains to St. Vitus Cathedral and interred them in the tomb that you now see. Designed by Viennese architect Fischer Von Erlach (who also designed the Clam-Gallus Palace in Old Town and which you might have seen on my Old Town Walk) and rendered by a Viennese silversmith named Wurth in the 1730s, John's tomb is made of – get this – **3,700 pounds of solid silver.** Understandably, there's usually a large crowd gathered here, and the railing around it creates quite a bottleneck, so if you encounter crowd, wait a bit to see if you get a clearing in the large numbers of people that congregate here. That way you can more comfortably take in this tomb and all of its cherubs and suspended angels, and you can also pay more attention to some of the other significant chapels next to it.

The Tomb of St. John of Nepomuk

Next to the Lady Chapel is the **Reliquary Chapel** (also known as the Saxon Chapel or the Sternberg Chapel) which contains the tombs of Přemysl Otakar I and Přemysl Otakar II, who each ruled in the 12th and 13th centuries. (Otakar II founded the town of Malá Strana as a settlement for German workers in 1257. At that time it was called New Town; the name was changed when King Charles founded the current New Town in the 14th century.) Both of these tombs were commissioned by King Charles IV in the 1370s and are also from Peter Parler's workshop.

Opposite St. John's tomb is the **Vlaším Chapel** (also known as the Chapel of St. John of Nepomuk or St. Adalbert's Chapel). It contains silver busts of SS. Adalbert, Wenceslas, Vitus and Cyril. Next is the **Waldstein Chapel** (or the Chapel of St. Mary Magdalene), just opposite another oak relief by Bechteler depicting a rampage through the Cathedral, where you'll find the tombs of both of the building's architects, **Matthias of Arras** and **Peter Parler**. It was rare at that time for "mere" architects to be honored in such a way. The tombstones are decorated with their portraits and are marked with plaques located at the base of each.

Next you'll come to the **Royal Oratory,** one of my favorite features of this structure. Here is some of the finest work of Benedikt Ried, the court architect to Vladislav II. Once you get to the Old Royal Palace, you'll see how Ried took the rather "radical" ribbing of Peter Parler a step further with his flower and star patterns in the ceiling of Vladislav Hall. His work in that building also starts to imitate nature in the way that the ribs of the ceiling twist and intertwine as they come down to form the columns, looking like tree trunks and branches, and here in the Royal Oratory he takes the theme of trees and branches to its peak. The realistic appearance of this stone carving, done by Hans Spies of Frankfurt in 1493, is superlative, and the overall effect is stunning.

Visible on the oratory are a couple of "Ws" for Vladislav (or Wladislaw in the Polish spelling of the king's name). One of the W's looks a lot like a McDonald's golden arch. And you'll also find an effigy of a miner from the town of Kutná Hora. This miner is dressed in typical miner's gear for the time, including a leather apron used for sliding down into the mines, and is holding a light source used for visibility. He's depicted on his knees on the mine's rocky floor, the usual position in effigies of Kutná Hora's miners. The shields on the Oratory are those of the lands ruled by Vladislav.

The next chapel after the Royal Oratory on the left as you walk west is the Chapel of the Holy Rood. From here there is a staircase that leads to the **Royal Crypt** (no longer open to the public) which contains the tombs of many Czech kings and queens, including Charles IV, Rudolf II and George of Poděbrady.

Next you'll take a peek at the most significant chapel in St. Vitus Cathedral: the **Chapel of St. Wenceslas.** It is the last chapel in the old part of the church on your left (south side of the building) just before the transept as you're continuing back toward the exit at the western end. As you approach it, you'll see the large Baroque **Monument of Count Schlick** on a pier opposite St. Wenceslas' Chapel. The bust of the Count was done by sculptor Matthias Braun.

It was King Charles' idea to place Wenceslas's chapel in this spot next to the transept and for his architect, Peter Parler, to place the main entrance to the church next to it, unusually, on the south side of the building. He wanted to give Wenceslas, his martyred ancestor, prominence as people entered the Cathedral. Charles did this in an attempt to unify his kingdom by glorifying Wenceslas. Wenceslas had been murdered in 935 by his brother, Boleslav, who hacked him to death.

The chapel walls are encrusted with approximately 1,345 semiprecious stones of Bohemian origin, including amethysts, set in gilded plaster. Wenceslas's remains were brought here and originally were interred in a solid gold casket – Charles' sons later sold the casket off in pieces. During his reign, King Charles had this chapel perpetually illuminated with 144 candles, the number of candles surely having been chosen because of some numerological significance (as was the number of stones) given numerology's importance in the mystical times of the 14th century.

There are two doorways through which you can view the chapel (if both of them are open – sometimes repairs cause one to be blocked off and closed). The first is on the left side of the southern aisle as you approach the

83

transept. From here you'll get a look at the current casket and some of the stones in the walls. In the far right corner, you'll see a small door that used to hold the Czech Crown Jewels. The window you see on the far wall behind the casket and to the left is a rather strange modern addition from 1968. After taking in the view from here, move around the corner to the left and look through the doorway in the western wall of the chapel, from which you'll get a view of the frescos on the far (eastern) wall depicting Charles and his fourth wife, Elizabeth of Pomerania, and Wenceslas and his wife, Jane of Bavaria, dating from the 14th to 16th centuries. And from this door, look to the left at the northern wall and take in the magnificent stones, especially the large amethysts, framing the door opening through which you just looked.

Now turn and continue making your way out of the Cathedral through the western end where you entered. On your way you'll pass three more 20th-century chapels on your left, including one funded by an insurance company that reads, "Those who Sow in Tears Shall Reap in Joy." When you exit the building back out into the **Third Courtyard,** turn left. If you are in need of a restroom, there's one here (on your left and to the right of the Cathedral as you face it). You'll need CZK 10 to use it.

As you walk toward the southern façade of St. Vitus, you'll pass the **Old Provost's Lodging.** This 17th-century Baroque building stands on the site of the original lodging which was a Romanesque palace.

View of Plečnik's obelisk and the Old Provost's Lodging
on the left

As you continue around to the south side of St. Vitus,
you'll pass an **obelisk.** It is the work of Josip Plečnik that
serves as a memorial to the fallen of WWI. Beyond it is a
statue of St. George slaying the dragon, the base of which
was also done by Plečnik. The Late-Gothic statue of St.
George is a copy of the original that was done in the late

14th century. Looking up from here at the Cathedral's 20th-century Neo-Gothic spires, the modern obelisk blends in well as a new addition.

The view of St. Vitus from the south side is truly spectacular. The place where the older 14th-century part of the structure ends with the soaring south-side tower is visible when compared with the more precisely cut stones of the newer part in the west, just past the tower to the left.

Southern facade of St. Vitus Cathedral

As I mentioned previously, the first St. Vitus church in the form of a rotunda was founded in 925 by Duke (now Saint) Wenceslas at the site where the Cathedral now stands. In 1060, a Romanesque basilica replaced the rotunda, which in turn was replaced by Charles's grand Gothic cathedral that you just toured. But at this spot between the Old Provost's Lodging and the Cathedral tower, remnants of the Romanesque basilica are visible through the grill running along the side of the building beneath a low roof.

Exposed Romanesque ruins of the 11th-century St. Vitus basilica

When Peter Parler died in 1399, his sons Johann and Wenzel continued work on the Cathedral, including the tower, until the Hussite Wars put an end to the construction. Later, when work resumed, Bonifaz Wohlmut completed the tower with a Renaissance top, and if you find some copies of older paintings of Prague, you'll see it in that form. In the 18th century, it was replaced with Picassi's Baroque dome which you see now. Thus, the tower contains Gothic, Baroque and Renaissance elements. The tower's height soars to 308 feet, and of the three Renaissance bells contained inside it, one, named the Sigismund Bell, is Bohemia's largest.

Note: You can climb the tower's steps to get magnificent views of Prague and the Castle, but a separate entry ticket is required.

On the south face of the tower is a huge Renaissance gold grille. Just above it is the letter "R." The "R" is for Rudolf, of course, Emperor Rudolph II, as it was he who had the grille installed and wanted everyone to know it was his doing.

Rudolf's Grille on the southern façade of St. Vitus

To the right (east) of the tower is what was meant to be (and what was originally and for several hundred years) the main entrance of the church, the so-called **Golden Portal.** The three sharply-pointed Gothic arches are topped by a beautiful mosaic of Christ at the **Last Judgement.** The mosaic was made with Bohemian glass by Venetian craftsmen. On the left, angels pull souls up from their graves and accompany them to heaven, while on the right some poor souls get sent back down to hell where the Devil awaits with his fire. King Charles and his fourth wife, Elizabeth of Pomerania, are also depicted on either side of Christ.

Detail of the Golden Portal mosaic

Unfortunately, the substances used to make the colors in the mosaic's tiles were chemically unstable; hence, they have altered and faded over time. In the 1990s, a restoration funded by the Getty Foundation was carried out, but the colors you see here now are as bright as they can get. Even faded, however, it is quite beautiful and impressive.

Tracery by Peter Parler under the southern entrance

Underneath the arches is more Gothic tracery by Peter Parler, the delicacy and intricacy of which highlights Parler's architectural skills. Now turn around to your right almost 180 degrees and you'll see Plečnik's **Bull Staircase** on the southeast end of the courtyard. Reminiscent of ancient temples in Minoa, this canopy made of copper and the accompanying staircase are a stroke of master design, and like much of Plečnik's work, look both modern and ancient at the same time.

Tip: If the Bull Staircase is open, it leads down to the **Garden on the Ramparts,** which offers more stunning views of Prague and the Malá Strana immediately below the Castle. You can pop down now for a quick look, or stroll through them at the end of this walk, depending on which way you exit the Castle when you finish. **Note, however, that the new security measures mean that, unfortunately, this stairway now seems to be closed more often than it used to be. If so, hopefully you can gain access to the garden from the Old Castle Steps.**

The Bull Staircase by Plečnik

Now we'll visit **Vladislav Hall** in the **Old Royal Palace,** which is located at the eastern end of the Third Courtyard just to the left of the Bull Staircase as you face it. The Old Royal Palace was the royal residence until the end of the 16th century. Vladislav Hall, which is located in the center of the structure, dates from the late 15th century and sits atop the old Gothic palace, which in turn sits atop the original Romanesque palace. The top floor contains the great hall. The hall is a marvel of architecture (or was in its day) and beauty. Enter the building, scan your ticket, then enter the door to the left of the turnstiles and you'll be standing in the hall.

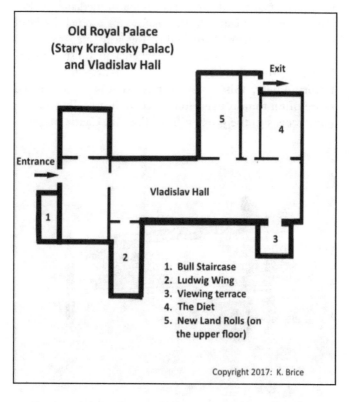

Old Royal Palace
(Stary Kralovsky Palac)
and Vladislav Hall

Exit

Entrance

Vladislav Hall

5

4

1

2

3

1. Bull Staircase
2. Ludwig Wing
3. Viewing terrace
4. The Diet
5. New Land Rolls (on
   the upper floor)

Copyright 2017: K. Brice

Designed by court architect Benedikt Ried for King

Vladislav II, Vladislav Hall, as I noted, is an architectural marvel of the Late Gothic. At the time it was built, it was the largest open space in Europe without any interior supports. With its five huge bays and large Renaissance windows, this space was awe-inspiring at the time (and still is).

The flower and star pattern of the ribbing in the ceiling vaults is a continuation of Parler's variations on ribbing in St. Vitus – Ried's design goes even further into decoration (form) than Parler's, while obviously being strong in function, as well, since it supports a ceiling over such a large, open space. It is so large, in fact, that jousting used to be practiced here, and waiters carried food into the hall on horseback for great banquets. Turn back and look at the door through which you entered the hall. You'll see that Ried has done some fancy work with the twisted columns which have been exposed on either side of the doorway, as well.

Now cross the room to the right (with the door through which you entered behind you and to your right) to the doorway on the south side of the room. This leads to the **Ludwig Wing** containing the Bohemian Chancellery – and the infamous window through which the **Second Defenestration of Prague** took place in 1618. The Second Defenestration is significant because it is credited with sparking the Thirty Years' War.

But before you reach the room where this window is located, you'll pass through another small room containing a model of the entire Prague Castle area, revealing the many layers of this district over its many centuries of existence.

Note: Along with the new security-mindedness at the Castle, this model has been recently roped off, so you can't get to all sides of it anymore. But you can still get a good look at the majority of the Castle structure.

It's especially interesting to see the original walls which were covered over by Maria Theresa's construction. On the model, the parts representing her architect's large edifice are made of clear plastic so that the original castle walls are visible underneath. The model's key also has all of the layers of the Castle color-coded by century ("stoleti" in Czech) so that you can better understand the Castle's development.

After perusing the model, continue to the next room where you'll find some great views of Prague out of the southern and eastern windows as well as some information about one of the most famous windows in Europe (the eastern one). As the placard explains, two Protestant nobles stormed the castle and threw two Catholic Governors and their clerk out of the window (in protest of the breaking of Rudolf's charter granting Protestants the right to worship and preach in Prague). Miraculously, all three survived the 50-foot plunge, in response to which the Catholic authorities, never missing a chance to promote the effectiveness of their faith, rounded up some local witnesses who swore they saw the Virgin Mary parachute the three to safety. In reality, though, it appears that a large garbage heap softened their fall, but nonetheless, this act eventually led to full-scale war.

If the Castle authorities have been kind enough to open the small window panes, take a look at the views (and take a few photos), then return to Vladislav Hall, taking note of the 17th-century Dutch ceramic stove that used to heat the Chancellery. When you reach the hall, turn right and continue toward the other end of the room (opposite from the end where you entered), stopping if you like to read the placard on the right that describes the many uses of the hall over the centuries, including the inauguration of all of the presidents of the Czech Republic and former Czechoslovakia (including the communist ones).

When you reach the other end of the hall (opposite from where you initially entered) you'll see a doorway on the right. If it's open, step through and enjoy more beautiful views from the open-air terrace.

Next cross the hall and enter the right-hand doorway at the northeast corner (also marked with twisted columns) on the opposite (northern) wall and enter the **Diet.** This room was designed by architect **Bonifaz Wohlmut** in the mid-16th century after Ried's original was destroyed in the fire of 1541, and it's immediately evident from the twisted columns bordering the doorway that Wohlmut was heavily influenced by Ried. Inside, Ried's influence continues in the Late Gothic star patterns in the ceiling vaults.

This chamber, which served as a parliament and throne room, is where the king would hold audiences with the noblemen of his various lands. On the walls are portraits of Austrian emperors and one empress, Maria Theresa, at the end of the row of paintings on the western wall, as well as a **copy of the Czech crown jewels** in a glass case on the right after you enter.

Note: At the time of this publication, the replica of the crown jewels had been moved for "technical reasons." However, the case is still there, so I assume they will return one day.

In the northwest corner is the Renaissance rostrum for the Clerk to the Diet, and the neo-Gothic tiled stove in the southwest is from 1836. The 19th-century throne is also neo-Gothic.

Leave this room and turn right. Walk past the first doorway on your right (which is actually the exit), and then turn right into the next doorway that leads to a spiral staircase. Take the stairs to the second floor and enter the **New Land Rolls.** Once upstairs, you'll eventually find yourself in room whose walls and ceiling are decorated with the crests of the clerks of the land registry who worked here from 1561-1774. Follow the arrows to the left, and in the far (southwest) corner, you'll see an original inscription bearing the name Vladislav in its Latin form ("Wladislawus") on what was originally an outer wall of Vladislav Hall before this wing was added. A peek out the window reveals the continuation of the original inscription.

Turn right and enter the room in which some sample land rolls are stored in a 16th-century cabinet, making a point to notice the beautiful door, hinges and lock of the entryway through which you pass. The cabinet on the far left contains some actual land rolls in books whose covers are hand-painted in bright colors. This addition to Vladislav Hall was originally built by Benedikt Ried, but after the fire of 1541 it was rebuilt by Wohlmut in the mid-16th century.

Pass through the third space on this level which contains copies of carved stone fragments from Ried's Vladislav Hall and the Diet. When you're ready to leave, return to the spiral staircase and Vladislav Hall. Then turn left and take the first left (the middle of the three doorways on the northern side of the hall) via the **Riders' Staircase.** This is where riders on horseback entered and exited the hall. You'll also note the point in the arch ahead, which was presumably meant to protect the riders' plumes atop their helmets as they passed under it. The shape and size of the stairs are built to accommodate a horse's gait, and you'll see more of Ried's beautiful vaulting in the staircase's ceiling.

View of St. Vitus from the east

When you exit the Old Royal Palace, you'll be on St. George's Square. Next you're headed for **St. George's Basilica** directly across the courtyard from you where you exit. But take some time as you approach it to turn back to your left and admire the impressive site of St. Vitus Cathedral and all of its buttresses from the back (eastern end). Note also just how narrow and high Peter Parler's center nave is, requiring all that complex buttressing to hold it up. Now turn yourself and your attention to St. George's opposite the back of St. Vitus.

The burnt orange Baroque façade in front of you dates to the 17th century; however, St. George's itself was begun in the 10th century and is the most well-preserved Romanesque church in Prague and the oldest surviving church at Prague Castle. The two white towers at the back are pure Romanesque. Enter by scanning your ticket and you'll find yourself inside the dark, narrow nave of this classically shaped basilica.

The Baroque façade of St. George's Basilica

Note: The term "basilica" originated in ancient Rome. The term at that time referred to both form and function. Basilicas were where Roman courts, or tribunes, were held, and they all had a distinct shape: a center nave with two side aisles and an apse at each end. Usually the emperor sat in one apse, and when Rome adopted Christianity, this shape was considered ideal for places of worship, with Christ at one end (or an altar), and thus the basilica was adopted as the basic shape of most churches for centuries to come. Today only certain dedicated Catholic churches are called basilicas.

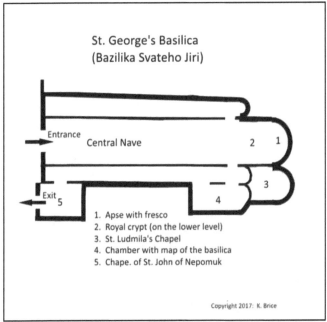

Detailed map of St. George's Basilica

Building techniques, materials and design in the Romanesque period did not allow for much in the way of either height or open spaces in walls. Therefore, the walls of St. George's Basilica are very thick and have very few window openings, and those openings that do exist are quite small. Likewise, most of the dividing wall between the main nave and the side aisles is made up of solid thick walls rather than columns topped by arches as would be the case in later Romanesque and then Gothic structures, and the width of the few columns in the basilica is quite large in proportion to their height when compared to those found in a Gothic structure. And of course, all of the arches found in St. George's (with the exception of those in St. Ludmila's chapel which was added later) are round rather than pointed, pointed arches being a Gothic feature (originating in the Middle East) that appeared later (and which supported more weight than the round arch, thus resulting in more light, space and height).

Walk along the left of the pews, noticing the uniquely Romanesque features of the building. At the opposite (eastern) end take the stairs leading up to the main altar. In the ceiling is a partially restored fresco. Its brilliant blue hues make one imagine just how impressive and colorful the fresco must have been when it was originally painted. To the right of the altar is **St. Ludmila's Chapel.** You'll note that it contains pointed Gothic arches, reflecting the fact that it was added later, in the 13th century.

Fresco in the apse of St. George's Basilica with St. Ludmila's Chapel on the right

Walk down the stairs on the right-hand side and continue turning right and down to the 12th-century crypt below the staircase. In here you'll find the original tympanum from the basilica. The statue on the right depicts the decaying body of a woman whose insides are being eaten by a creepy-crawly creature. Some say she depicts a woman murdered by her lover, and this was the state in which her body was found in the Stag Moat that you crossed if you began this walk at one of the first two starting points, but no one is sure. More likely it is a representation of Vanitas, a genre of art symbolizing the worthlessness of earthly goods and the inevitability of death.

Now go back up the stairs and enter the right (southern) side aisle of the Basilica, noting the exposed brick at the eastern end which reveals the details of how arches and semicircular domes were created. Further to the right of the side aisle is a small chamber with a plaque containing some information about St. George's Basilica in several languages, including English, and on the western wall there is a color-coded architectural diagram showing when various parts of the basilica were built, repaired or added, from the 10th century all the way to the 18th (the Chapel of St. John of Nepomuk through which you'll pass when you exit). From the diagram, however, you can see that most of the structure dates from the 10th to the 12th centuries, making this one of the oldest buildings in Prague.

Now walk down the northern aisle. You'll pass by several tombstones hanging on the wall on your left with accompanying diagrams on your right of the archeological digs that revealed the graves beneath them. You'll exit through the Baroque **Chapel of St. John of Nepomuk,** but the bones displayed in the reliquary under the altar are not those of St. John (his are in his silver tomb in St. Vitus Cathedral). Rather, these are apparently the bones of an abbess. The frescoes in the chapel are by Václav Reiner, while the chapel itself was designed by František Kaňka.

The sculptor Ferdinand Brokoff did the statue of St. John above the entrance.

Tip: Ferdinand Brokoff was from a family of Bohemian sculptors. He was a contemporary of Matthias Braun, who is widely considered the greatest Bohemian Baroque sculptor, while Ferdinand is considered the best sculptor of the Brokoff family. For some exquisite examples of both Braun's and Ferdinand Brokoff's work in Prague, see my Malá Strana and Old Town walks (Chapter 9). Also featured in my Malá Strana walk is the Vrtba Garden, on which Kaňka, Reiner and Braun collaborated.

When you exit the basilica, you'll again be presented with a photo op of the rear of the Cathedral. Take some shots and then turn to your left 180 degrees and walk down St. George's Lane (Jiřská) to the right of the basilica with the Cathedral at your back. As you walk past St. George's, notice the fine carving in the Renaissance southern entry to the basilica.

Carving over the southern entry to St. George's Basilica

Next you'll visit the **Golden Lane.** Look for an

opening on the left just past St. George's and follow the signs.

Tip: If you're a fan of Christmas, or more specifically, of Christmas ornaments, you might want to take a short detour and check out the little shop just past the opening that leads to Golden Lane. This shop is open year-round and has nothing but Christmas decorations, mainly hand-blown, hand-painted Czech Christmas tree ornaments. They are of quite good quality and interesting design, and the prices aren't bad either. Don't worry about breakage – just tell them that you're taking a flight and need them wrapped well. They do a pretty good job of packaging.

As with everything in Prague, there are many theories as to how Golden Lane got its name. Some say it's because it was once lined with the shops of goldsmiths – or with Rudolf's alchemists (in reality, the alchemists' laboratories were located in the Mihulka, or Powder, Tower of the Castle). Another theory suggests that it was because of the golden color of the narrow street in the mornings when the bedpans were emptied. In any case, this charming lane was created by the construction of the fortress walls in the late 15th century and was later lined with tiny houses of varying shapes and sizes in 1597 by Rudolf II for his guards. Later, servants and various craftspeople who served the Castle and its environs occupied these spaces, and the lane still had residents until the 1950s. The influential Czech writer Franz Kafka lived in number 22 for a short time (from 1912-14), and it was here that he wrote "A Country Doctor." You can purchase a copy of this and other of his works in the bookshop that now occupies this space.

Currently, most of the other buildings on Golden Lane have been converted into period shops and quarters, such as the home of a seamstress or the home of a candle maker or an herbalist, while the remainder have been converted into cute little souvenir shops where you can purchase marionettes and more. At the far end of the lane to the left after you pass through the entry turnstiles is some old battle artillery on display. And if you like old weaponry, armor and/or torture instruments, you can visit the display in the upper floor wall-walk above the houses lining the lane. Follow the signs in the row of houses just to the left of the turnstiles where you scanned your ticket.

There's only one way out of Golden Lane, and that route will take you past **Dalibor's Tower (Daliborka),** the last official site on your short visit ticket. The tower (and parts of the wall behind the houses on Golden Lane) was designed by Benedikt Ried who was the architect of Vladislav Hall that you saw earlier. Demonstrating Ried's versatility when it came to both function and style, these 15th-century fortifications reveal that he was adept at designing massive structures, too.

Dalibor's Tower served as a prison for white collar criminals, whose punishment was being lowered into a chamber located underneath the dungeon with its massive vaults where they were basically left to starve to death and rot. The tower was completed in 1496 and served as a prison until 1781. It gets its name from its first inmate, Dalibor of Kozojedy.

Note: The name "Kozojedy" roughly translates to "goat eaters." Many (perhaps most) Czech towns and villages have names that, when translated into English, at least, render some funny results given the non-literal nature of the names of most English towns and cities. Some examples are Lednice ("refrigerator"), Hrdlořezy ("throat cutters"), and my personal favorite, Skoronice ("almost-nothing-ville"). The neighborhoods of Prague are no different. Try your luck and skill at translating the names of some of the city's metro stations and see what you come up with.

And Czech surnames are similar. After living here for so many years and meeting people with names like Mrs. "Not-At-Home" or Mr. "No Time" or Mr. "Cute Little Fat Man," I thought I had heard it all. But recently I met someone named Mr. "Emergency." That took the cake!

Dalibor was imprisoned in the tower in the late 15th century for failing to resist a serf uprising and then sheltering the offending rebels on his premises. Legend says he learned to play violin in the tower, and Czech composer Bedrich Smetana composed an opera bearing his name. But while the opera does exist, the story about Dalibor learning to play the violin while imprisoned is truly just legend – or myth. The violin had not yet been invented.

Entrance to Dalibor's Tower

To visit the tower, turn left once you've descended the steps that take you out of the eastern end of Golden Lane (watch your head and your step – the ceiling is low and the stairs are uneven). You will be on the edge of the Castle grounds, with views of the Old Town off to the right. Turn left and enter the tower. After descending the first set of stairs, you'll see a small door opening in the wall on the left. This leads to another **very** narrow (one-way traffic only) staircase that takes you down to the chamber containing a hole in the floor through which prisoners were lowered. It also contains a holding cell, a chopping block complete with a bucket for catching severed heads, and other torture instruments that are truly disturbing when you imagine their uses.

On the same level off of which you entered the door to the small stairway is a room directly ahead containing yet more torture instruments, as well as some info in English about the tower.

And, on that cheerful note...! This is the end of the Castle walk. Once you've exited the tower, as with Golden Lane, there is only one way out (just like the Allman Brothers' song). With the tower behind you and the views of Old Town in front of you and slightly to the left, take the stairway on the right up to a large courtyard with a raised platform, again on the right. Ahead you'll see a statue of a nude adolescent boy. You'll be facing his backside, and as you pass in front of him headed for the exit gate that is also in front of him, you'll notice that one particular part of his anatomy is very well polished indeed. Pause for a photo if you wish and then exit the gate the boy is facing. From here you have several choices for exiting the Castle.

Tip: Immediately in front of you across the lane when you exit the gate mentioned above, you'll see the Lobkowicz Palace. In addition to a visit to the Lobkowicz Collections being listed in my Prague guidebook in the chapter titled "A Few of My Favorite Things," the

Lobkowicz Café is a great place to have lunch if you're hungry, which you probably are by this point. Pass through the palace's entry and into a courtyard. Here you'll be able to dine outdoors in warmer months. If it's raining or cold, continue inside to the café. It also boasts a wonderful balcony where you can dine – again, if weather permits – and enjoy splendid views of Prague. The balcony is usually full, as it is highly sought-after and is now listed in most guidebooks, but you might get lucky. In any case, the food is quite good here (try the crinkle fries), and their apple strudel with whipped cream is tops. The hot chocolate isn't bad, either, especially on a cold day.

After lunch, you can tour the collections if you wish (especially a good thing to do if it happens to be raining), and be sure to use the audio guide that is included in the price of your entry ticket. The Lobkowicz Palace is privately-owned; thus, a separate entry ticket in addition to your Castle ticket is required. Still, it's a bargain for what you'll see, and the audio guide is narrated by Prince William Lobkowicz himself, adding a personal touch to the art and family heirlooms in the collection. And even though he's a prince, William is American – it's a good story, and he tells it well.

Now, back to the various Castle exits... One possibility is to turn left (with the statue of the boy at your back) and walk downhill, with the **Lobkowicz Palace** on your right. You will pass through the Castle's eastern gate, getting one more chance to take photos of or with the Castle Guards. You can continue straight down the **Old Castle Steps (Starý Zámecké Schody),** stopping to observe the views of town on the right where you'll see throngs of others doing the same. When you get to the bottom of the steps, turn right and walk along the street (Klárov) until you reach the Malostranská metro station and tram stop. Here you can get the green ("A") metro line or the 2, 12, 15, 18, 20 and 22 trams.

Another option is to eschew the Old Castle Stairs and turn right almost 180 degrees after you pass the Castle Guards and walk along the **Garden on the Ramparts** which I mentioned earlier when I pointed out the Bull Staircase. You can visit the gardens and turn around and exit as described above, or you can continue in the garden all the way back to Hradčanské Náměstí and the Castle Gates. From here, you have two choices. Once you ascend the stairs at the (western) end of the gardens, turn sharply to the left almost 180 degrees and walk down to the Malá Strana via the **Castle Steps (Zámecké Schody).** This will take you back down close to Malostranské Náměstí where you can get trams 12, 15, 20 or 22.

The Castle Steps (Zámecké Schody)

Or, at the top of the western stairs of the Garden on the Ramparts, continue straight ahead, with Starbucks on your left, and walk down to Malostranské Náměstí via the famous Nerudova Street. As you begin your descent on Ke Hradu, you'll come to a point where the road and the crowds will do a hairpin turn back to the left. This is Nerudova. Continue downhill until you reach the square (náměstí).

Note: Because of security, the western gates to the Garden on the Ramparts might be locked, which means that the only route out from here would be back via the Old Castle Steps as described above. This is constantly changing, so unfortunately I can't promise how it will be when you visit.

Finally, after you exit from the courtyard with the boy statue you can turn right on Jiřská Street and walk uphill, past the Christmas shop, toward the Cathedral and exit via Prašný Most and take the tram (22) back downhill. Or you can exit via the First Courtyard and Hradčanské Náměstí and walk downhill via Nerudova Street or the Castle Steps as described above.

I hope you've enjoyed my Prague Castle Walk!

9 CONTACT

Thank you for purchasing my book! I hope you enjoyed your walk through Prague Castle. If you'd like more information on this amazing city, including great dining, shopping and transport information, please see my guidebook: **"Prague Travel Tips: An American's Guide to Her Adopted City."** It's available on Amazon.com, in bookstores and on my website: www.exclusivepraguetours.com/guidebooks.

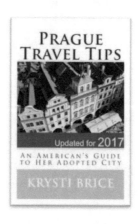

You might also enjoy my other guided walks: **"Prague Self-Guided Walks: Old Town," "Prague Self-Guided Walks: The Lesser Quarter,"** and **"Prague Self-Guided Walks: The Jewish Quarter."**

They're also available on Amazon.com, in bookstores (you might have to have them ordered) and on my website: www.pragueguidebook.weebly.com/prague-self-guided-walks.

My Prague Restaurant Guide

If you're a foodie headed to Prague or if you just want a good meal at a good price, my restaurant guide will steer you in the right direction!

Prague is going through a new revolution - a food revolution - and there is some excellent food to be had here, Czech or otherwise. You'll find the best places listed in my book!

Private Guided Tours – Your Interests, Your Pace

For almost a decade now, I've provided private guided tours of Prague to discerning travelers of all stripes and ages. My tours are **tailored to your interests and pace,** and in addition to showing you the most significant historical sites of this city, I'll also point out the best places to eat and shop and will show you how to get around the city so that you can explore more in-depth on your own. On my tours, I will take you off the beaten path as much as possible, while helping you make the most of your time in Prague.

I'd be delighted to meet you and give you a **personal introduction** to this city that I still find amazing after all these years.

Day Trips to Kutná Hora

I also offer day trips to the historical town of Kutná Hora, should you be interested in exploring the Czech Republic beyond Prague. Kutná Hora, a UNESCO site, is a beautiful medieval, mostly Gothic, city, with many historical landmarks revealing its rich silver mining past. It is one of my favorite places and is highly recommended. In addition to the historical structures, the town itself offers stunning views of its small valley from the "hora" (small mountain). There is also a wonderful art gallery there and a good place to have lunch. The picture below is from the Avenue of Statues in Kutná Hora.

So, if you're interested in a private tour, please contact me at: **krysti.brice@seznam.cz** or through my website at: **www.exclusivepraguetours.com.**

Concierge Services – Make the Most of Your Time in Prague

In any foreign country, making arrangements and plans can be a challenge. And in the Czech Republic, given the difficulty of the Czech language and the not-always-helpful or forthcoming customer service, it can be downright daunting. Under my "Concierge Services," I offer travel advice and assistance, saving you time, energy and perhaps money, too. The following photo is from the interior of the Municipal House, a beautiful Art Nouveau musical venue.

So, if you want help getting concert or train information, buying your tickets or making restaurant recommendations/reservations, I can do all that for you and save you time spent surfing the web. More details can be found on my website:

www.exclusivepraguetours.com/concierge.

Discount Shopping Coupons

The Czech Republic is known for its fine cut crystal and glass, as well as garnets, which are mined in the town of Turnov. I can give you coupons entitling you to a discount (of up to 15-23% depending on how much you spend) at Prague's best crystal and garnet shop.

Contact me at: krysti.brice@seznam.cz or through my website at www.exclusivepraguetours.com and I will be happy to mail some to you or deliver them to your hotel.

Hotel Offers

In case you have not yet chosen a hotel in Prague, I can offer discounted rates, free breakfast (a $20 per person, per day value) and free upgrades (subject to availability) to my clients at Prague's luxury Grand Mark Hotel, a member of the Leading Hotels of the World group. The Grand Mark is one of Prague's top luxury hotels and is in a great location – perfect for beginning a tour of Old Town. The Mark is also very close to Prague's main train station and is around the corner from a local train station. A metro (subway) stop is a block away, and there are several tram stops only a block or two from the hotel at various places. You can see photos of the Mark on my website at the link below. Let me know if you would like me to check rates for you.

www.exclusivepraguetours.com/hotels.html

Facebook and More

And finally, if you're on Facebook, check out my Tour Page to see great photos of Prague and get up-to-date information. And I would love it if you would "Like" my page: www.facebook.com/ExclusivePragueTours.

Thanks, and I wish you a great time in Prague!

Krysti

Notes

ABOUT THE AUTHOR

Krysti Brice, a native of Macon, Georgia, and a graduate of New York University, is a former CPA and investment banker who began her career at Deloitte in New York City. In 1992, she moved to Prague where she continued her work at Deloitte as an adviser to the Ministry of Privatization. While in Prague, she joined the World Bank and was based in both Prague and Washington, DC. After ten years with the Bank and three years in Washington, she returned to Prague in 2000, where she now works as an author, mentor and guide to the city.

Made in United States
Troutdale, OR
12/01/2023